I KNOW WHAT TO DO! SOCIAL SKILLS

HOW TO BE A GOOD FRIEND

CAITIE MCANENEY

PowerKiDS press

Published in 2025 by The Rosen Publishing Group, Inc.
2544 Clinton Street, Buffalo, NY 14224

First Edition

Editor: Caitie McAneney
Book Design: Rachel Rising

Photo Credits: Cover, pp. 1, 7 Monkey Business Images/Shutterstock.com; pp. 4-6, 8, 10, 12, 14, 16, 18, 20 Cute art/Shutterstock.com; p. 5 wavebreakmedia/Shutterstock.com; p. 9 PeopleImages.com - Yuri A/Shutterstock.com; p. 11 Hryshchyshen Serhii/Shutterstock.com; p. 13 NDAB Creativity/Shutterstock.com; p. 15 Veja/Shutterstock.com; p. 17 Sergey Novikov/Shutterstock.com; p. 19 metamorworks/Shutterstock.com; p. 21 YanLev Alexey/Shutterstock.com.

Library of Congress Cataloging-in-Publication Data

Names: McAneney, Caitie, author.
Title: How to be a good friend / Caitie McAneney.
Description: Buffalo, NY : PowerKids Press, [2025] | Series: I know what to do! Social skills | Includes bibliographical references and index.
Identifiers: LCCN 2024028800 (print) | LCCN 2024028801 (ebook) | ISBN 9781499450453 (library binding) | ISBN 9781499450446 (paperback) | ISBN 9781499450460 (ebook)
Subjects: LCSH: Friendship in children–Juvenile literature. | Friendship–Juvenile literature.
Classification: LCC BF723.F68 M323 2025 (print) | LCC BF723.F68 (ebook) | DDC 177/.62–dc23/eng/20240705
LC record available at https://lccn.loc.gov/2024028800
LC ebook record available at https://lccn.loc.gov/2024028801

Manufactured in the United States of America

CPSIA Compliance Information: Batch #CWPK25. For Further Information contact Rosen Publishing at 1-800-237-9932.

CONTENTS

Making Friends

You start a new school. You join a new team. You move. You want to make friends. It can feel hard! You may feel shy or **anxious**. Look around at people your age. Who seems friendly? You can ask to sit with them. You can ask to play.

PRACTICE MAKES PROGRESS!

To make friends, you can say:

"Hi! My name is ______."

"Can I sit with you?"

"Can I play too?"

"I like dinosaurs too."

Including Others

How can you be a good friend? You can ask others to play. You can **invite** them to sit with you. You can include them in a game. Maybe a kid is new to school. You can say, "Come play with us!"

Celebrating Differences

Everyone is different! Some kids are tall. Some kids are short. Some kids have glasses. Some kids have hair or skin that is different from yours. Some kids speak a different language. That's cool! You can still play together. Celebrate **diversity**!

Playtime!

You can be a good friend when you play. Your friend may want to play one way. You want to play another way. That's okay! There is no wrong way to play. You can listen to each other. Then you can decide to play apart or together.

Kindness Counts

Good friends are kind! They use kind words. They say "please" and "thank you." They give **compliments**. They might say, "I love your singing voice!" or "Cool shirt!" Kind people act with fairness and **generosity**. They make others feel good.

Here to Listen

Good friends listen to others. Your friend may feel sad or mad. You can **support** them. You can care about their feelings. They may need someone to talk to. You can ask, "Want to talk about it?" You can also just sit with them.

Taking Turns

It's good to take turns. There is only one kite. You and your friend want to use it. You can go one at a time. You can say, "You go first. Then I'll go!" You can share toys, too. Sharing is caring!

Handling Fights

Sometimes friends fight. You can practice being a good friend. First, take time and space to calm down. Take deep breaths. Then go to your friend. Tell them how you feel. Maybe you need to say you are sorry. Then they might want to play again!

Keeping Friends

Many friends share the same interests. For example, your friend may love swimming—just like you! Playing may seem easy. But friendships take work! Some friendships last for a school year. Some last for a long time. Being a good friend will keep your friendships strong.

GLOSSARY

anxious: Feeling worried about something.

compliment: Something good that you say about someone.

diversity: The state of having many different kinds.

generosity: Willing to give what one has.

invite: To ask someone to go somewhere or do something.

support: To help during a time of trouble.

FOR MORE INFORMATION

BOOKS

Borgert-Spaniol, Megan. *Friends Support Each Other*. Oxford, UK: Raintree Publishers, 2023.

Peters, Katie. *I Care for My Friend*. Minneapolis, MN: Lerner Publications, 2023.

WEBSITES

How to Be an Awesome Friend
kids.nationalgeographic.com/pages/article/friend
Read this article for great tips on how to be an awesome friend.

PBS Kids Talk About: Friendship
ny.pbslearningmedia.org/resource/pkta-friendship-media/pbs-kids-talk-about-media-gallery/
Listen to kids just like you talk about friendship!

Publisher's note to educators and parents: Our editors have carefully reviewed these websites to ensure that they are suitable for students. Many websites change frequently, however, and we cannot guarantee that a site's future contents will continue to meet our high standards of quality and educational value. Be advised that students should be closely supervised whenever they access the internet.

INDEX